HEINEMANN Profiles

Rupert Murdoch

An Unauthorized Biography

Andrew Langley

Heinemann
LIBRARY

www.heinemann.co.uk
Visit our website to find out more information about **Heinemann Library** books.

To order:
☎ Phone 44 (0) 1865 888066
▤ Send a fax to 44 (0) 1865 314091
▢ Visit the Heinemann Bookshop at www.heinemann.co.uk to browse our catalogue
and order online.

First published in Great Britain by Heinemann Library, Halley Court, Jordan Hill, Oxford
OX2 8EJ, a division of Reed Educational and Professional Publishing Ltd.
Heinemann is a registered trademark of Reed Educational & Professional Publishing Limited.

OXFORD MELBOURNE AUCKLAND JOHANNESBURG BLANTYRE GABORONE
IBADAN PORTSMOUTH NH (USA) CHICAGO

Produced for Heinemann Library by Discovery Books Limited
Designed by Barry Dwyer
Originated by Dot Gradations
Printed and bound in Hong Kong/China

ISBN 0 431 08645 1 (hardback)
05 04 03 02 01
10 9 8 7 6 5 4 3 2 1

British Library Cataloguing in Publication Data

Langley, Andrew
Rupert Murdoch. – (Heinemann Profiles)
1. Murdoch, Rupert, 1931- – Juvenile literature 2. Newspapers – Ownership – Biography – Juvenile literature 3. Newspaper publishing – Australia – Biography – Juvenile Literature 4. Mass media – Biography – Juvenile literature
I. Title
338.7'61'0701'092

Acknowledgements
The Publishers would like to thank the following for permission to reproduce photographs:
Aquarius p39; Corbis pp4 (& sidebar) (Roger Ressmeyer), 17 & 31 (top & bottom) (Bettmann), 23 & 34
(Hulton-Deutsch Collection), 53 (Reuters NewMedia Inc.); Eye Ubiquitous p10 (L. Fordyce); Hulton Getty
pp12, 18; John Frost Newspapers pp24, 27, 29; Panos p44; Popperfoto pp9, 21, 37; Popperfoto/Reuters pp7,
15, 35, 41, 42, 47, 48, 51; Rex pp33, 40.

Cover photograph reproduced with permission of Corbis (Mitchell Gerber)

Every effort has been made to contact copyright holders of any material reproduced in this book. Any
omissions will be rectified in subsequent printings if notice is given to the Publisher.

Any words appearing in the text in bold, **like this**, are explained in the Glossary.

CONTENTS

WHO IS RUPERT MURDOCH?

Rupert Murdoch is one of the most powerful businesspeople of the age. He owns newspapers, TV stations, book publishers, a film company and dozens of other massive businesses all over the world. His **holding company**, News Corporation Limited, has a world-wide grip on the way we are informed and entertained.

News Corporation is based on the traditional news media – ones which use the written word. Its newspapers are read across the world. They range from the weighty and serious London *Times* to many local newspapers in the United States, Australia and elsewhere. Murdoch has always appointed **editors** who could be sure of grabbing the public's attention.

Murdoch in front of the printing presses of the New York Post, one of his many newspapers.

They in turn have developed a new kind of popular paper. Hard news has often given way to crude and sensational stories about famous people. Scandal, competitions and sport dominate the pages, along with frequent photographs of topless girls. But these aggressive methods work. The sales of most Murdoch newspapers have soared past their rivals.

Murdoch also realized, early in his career, that new technology was going to become vital to the future of the media. So he gained control of television channels, and launched **satellite** and **digital TV** services such as BSkyB. It seemed a big risk, but he has always stayed one step ahead of his competitors.

Murdoch has built up his huge empire through a mixture of luck, boldness and – above all – ruthless energy. Driven on by fierce ambition, he has devoted his life to his work. As a result, he has had little time to relax, and he has few outside interests. He rarely reads books or listens to music, sleeps badly and has had several health scares.

FIRST YEARS IN AUSTRALIA

Rupert Murdoch was born on 11 March 1931 near Melbourne, Australia to a wealthy family. With his three sisters, Anne, Helen and Janet, he grew up in a roomy country house close to the sea. There was plenty of land and a huge garden to wander in, complete with a tennis court and stables full of ponies.

NEWSPAPERS IN THE BLOOD

It was a remarkable family. Murdoch's two grandfathers could not have been more different – one was an upright minister of the church, while the other was a wild gambler. His mother, Elisabeth, was anxious that her children should not be spoilt by wealth. She even insisted that young Rupert sleep in a tree house throughout each summer to make him tough and self-reliant.

Murdoch's father was an even stronger influence. Sir Keith Murdoch ran a chain of newspapers and radio

'He had no time for imaginary things, fairy tales and so on. He liked links with reality.'
Dame Elisabeth Murdoch
on her son, 1984.

stations across Australia. He was a friend of prime ministers and other powerful people. But above all he was remembered as a fearless front-line reporter during the First World War, and a national hero.

Making money

Murdoch worshipped his father, and tried hard to please him. He soon shared Sir Keith's love for the world of newspapers, and often visited him at work in the offices of the *Melbourne Herald*. The thunder of the presses and the air of excitement there thrilled him deeply.

He also learned very early how to make money. With his sister Helen, he would trap rabbits and other small animals in the nearby countryside. He paid his sister one penny an animal for the mucky job of skinning them – then sold the skins for sixpence each!

OFF TO SCHOOL

At eleven years old, Rupert was sent to a **boarding school**. This was Geelong Grammar, a school for the sons of wealthy families set on the rugged shores of Victoria. Life there was tough. The boys had cold showers every morning (even in winter) and were expected to wash dishes and dig the gardens as well as attend lessons and take part in sport.

Murdoch hated it at first. He disliked team sports, and rebelled against Geelong's rigid rules. Some boys bullied him because of his father's powerful position. He felt like an outsider.

But he quickly found ways to enjoy himself. He bought a motorbike, which he hid near the school and used for trips to the nearest race course. He acted in the Geelong drama productions. He became a leading speaker in the school's debating society, and argued in favour of many unpopular causes, such as **trade unions** and taking banks out of private hands.

A FIRST TASTE OF JOURNALISM

In 1947, Murdoch passed his school exams. However, he was still too young to leave, and stayed at Geelong for another year. He now had time to start his first magazine. It gave everyone in the school, he said, 'an opportunity to air their opinions'. There were essays on many topics, including amongst other things modern art, **socialism** and **racism** in Australia.

Leaving Geelong at last, Murdoch tried his hand at real journalism. His father arranged a job for him on the *Melbourne Herald* as a **cub reporter**, the bottom rung of the newspaper ladder. For a few months, Murdoch covered stories about the police and the law courts.

Collins Street in Melbourne as the young Rupert Murdoch would have seen it.

A TASTE OF BRITISH LIFE

Murdoch made his first trip to Britain in 1950. He had a place at Oxford University, but first there was a summer job to do. This took him to Birmingham, where he worked on the local newspaper, the *Gazette*, for a few months. When he left, he wrote to the *Gazette*'s owner and urged him to sack the **editor**!

AN AUSSIE AT OXFORD

That autumn, Murdoch settled into his room in Worcester College, Oxford. He studied Politics, Philosophy and Economics, but study often bored him. He preferred enjoying himself at the university clubs and on trips to the race course.

The grand frontage of Worcester College, Oxford.

Many other students found Murdoch difficult to like. He was rich and noisy, and did not hide his scorn for the English **class system** and its snooty ways. Worse still, he also had a lot of **left-wing** views which did not seem to fit in with his big-spending lifestyle. As a result, when he tried to join an Oxford cricket team or become a club secretary, he was turned down.

TRAVEL AND TRAGEDY

There was plenty of excitement outside college walls. Murdoch visited friends throughout England – once arriving in a brand-new Rolls Royce which he had borrowed on a promise to write about it in a Murdoch paper. He also made trips to Paris and other European cities which boasted good casinos.

Keith Murdoch, by this time very ill, was worried by his son's behaviour. He desperately wanted him to take on his newspaper empire. When Sir Keith died in October 1952, Rupert took the first plane home. Even so, to his great sorrow he missed the funeral.

Turbulent, travelled and twenty-one, he is known as a brilliant betting man.'
Cherwell student magazine on Murdoch, 1952.

Learning the trade

Sir Keith had not been hugely wealthy. He left his son **shares** in the newspapers in Brisbane and Adelaide and little else, although he wished (in his will) that Rupert should have 'a useful and full life in newspaper and broadcasting activities'. That is exactly what Rupert Murdoch wanted, too.

Murdoch took his final Oxford exams in 1953 and gained only a third-class degree. His eye was now firmly on his future – in newspapers. But before returning to Australia, he was determined to learn about the craft of journalism. He took a job on the *Daily Express* in London.

Sub-editors hard at work in 1950s' Fleet Street.

This was an ideal training ground. The *Daily Express* was then one of the brightest and best-run papers in the world. Murdoch worked as a **sub-editor**, polishing the journalists' copy and writing snappy **headlines**. His experiences here gave him practical ideas about how a newspaper should be run.

HOME AT LAST

The 22-year-old Murdoch flew home late in 1953 to take up the challenge of his family business. This was based in Adelaide, the capital city of South Australia. Here the Murdoch-run papers, the *Adelaide News* and the *Sunday Mail*, had to compete with the more powerful *Adelaide Advertiser*. The new boss had to plunge straight into the first big battle of his business life.

'Please don't get the impression that I will be walking in [and telling] you what's wrong with everything. I will be treading softly for a time.'

Rupert Murdoch in a letter to the *Adelaide News* editor, 1953.

Start of an Australian Empire

Whatever he promised, Murdoch could not resist making his presence felt in the Adelaide offices. He began to pick out the faults in his newspapers. The **layouts** were dull, stories were lazily written, there were not enough pictures. He tried to cut costs by keeping as small a staff as possible. And it worked. Slowly, the re-shaped *Adelaide News* started to sell more copies.

Struggle for the sundays

But his biggest headache was the *Adelaide Advertiser*. The owners of the city's rival daily paper were clearly determined to put him out of business and force him to sell up. They had just launched a Sunday newspaper to compete with Murdoch's *Sunday Mail*. There was not room in Adelaide for both, so one would have to surrender.

The fierce battle lasted for more than two years. But the *Sunday Mail* had a faithful **readership**, and the *Adelaide Advertiser* lost money fast. In the end, the two owners agreed to merge their weekend papers, each taking a 50 per cent share.

First marriage

For all his brashness at work, the young Murdoch was often awkward and shy with girls. But when he met Pat Booker, a blonde air hostess from Melbourne, he made up his mind to marry her. She taught him to dance, and he in turn taught her to bet on horseraces.

Their wedding took place in Adelaide in March 1956 (it was reported in the *Adelaide Advertiser*, but not in Murdoch's own *Adelaide News*). A daughter, Prudence, was born three years later.

Murdoch at the wedding of his eldest daughter Prudence to Crispin Odey in 1985.

But Murdoch's burning ambition and dedication to his empire took up most of his time. By the 1960s, he was spending most of the year apart from his wife and they were divorced in 1967.

Expanding the empire

The profits from the *Adelaide News* steadily rose. By 1956, Murdoch could look for new publishing ventures outside Adelaide. He bought *New Idea*, a women's weekly magazine from Melbourne, and a third newspaper, the *Perth Sunday Times*.

This was a quiet weekend paper, with a falling **readership**. Murdoch flung himself into the task of spicing it up. The paper was filled with lurid headlines, exaggerated gossip and startling pictures. The sensational Murdoch style had arrived.

Launch into television

Murdoch was encouraged, and bought more newspapers. Many of these were small concerns in the more isolated corners of Australia, such as the *Northern Territory News* and the *Barrier Miner*, but they all added to his grip on national journalism.

All the same, he now turned his attention to an even more powerful medium – television. He had made several visits to the USA, where he toured TV stations and looked at possible programmes to buy. In 1957 he applied for one of two **licences** to run new **commercial** channels serving Adelaide.

'As a newspaper man, you had to be in television to protect your position.'
Murdoch interview, 1957.

GOING ON AIR

Once again, Murdoch was up against his powerful rivals at the *Adelaide Advertiser*, which also owned broadcasting stations. He was granted Channel 9, while they had Channel 7. Another frantic race began, to see who would be ready to go on air first. Driven on by its boss, Channel 9 won and was ready for launch late in 1959. It was an instant hit, and drew in vast amounts of advertisers' money.

FIGHTING FOR CONTROL

By the end of the 1950s, Murdoch was eager for a new challenge. He now moved into the cut-throat world of Sydney newspapers. Sydney is the largest city in Australia and Murdoch knew he had joined a much bigger league. Here, he had not just one but two powerful rivals – the Packer family and the Fairfax family.

Murdoch shows off the new-look Sydney *Daily Mirror* in May 1960.

The Packers and Fairfaxes did not see the newcomer as a threat at first. Fairfax even agreed to sell Murdoch two of his newspapers, the *Daily* and *Sunday Mirror*. He was glad to get rid of them, for they were both losing money and readers fast.

Murdoch also had his sights set on a printing company in Sydney. This small, but well-equipped, firm was up for sale, and the owner offered it to Murdoch. The Packers, meanwhile, were determined to have the company for themselves.

One night in 1960, a gang of Packer employees broke into the building and began to change the locks. Someone tipped off Murdoch, who assembled a gang and rushed to the rescue. By early next morning they had thrown out the invaders.

CIRCULATION BATTLE

Murdoch now had the papers, the printers and a company to distribute his wares. His next aim was to sell more copies. In the newspaper world this is known as increasing circulation. To achieve this he used the simplest possible methods – more sensational journalism and much heavier promotion.

The *Sunday Mirror*'s **headlines** grew larger and more shocking while the stories became cheekier. Murdoch urged his editors to use more pictures of women in bathing suits. When the papers ran competitions, they had to offer bigger and better prizes than their Sydney rivals. As before, this explosive new mixture worked, and the number of readers soared.

A BRAND NEW PAPER

Canberra is the capital city of Australia. In the early 1960s it was growing at huge speed. It had only one daily newspaper, the *Canberra Times*, and Murdoch believed there was room for a second.

He quietly bought a piece of land near the *Times* offices. When the *Times* owner asked him what he wanted it for, Murdoch replied, 'To run you out of town'. Then he finalized his plans for a new daily.

But his plans had to change. The owner of the *Canberra Times* was alarmed, and spent a vast sum to update and enlarge his newspaper. Murdoch wisely realized that he could not compete. So he decided to publish a national newspaper.

GOING NATIONWIDE

There were enormous difficulties to overcome. Worldwide news stories had to be gathered. Advertisers had to be charmed. Agents had to be found to distribute the paper on time to the state capitals. The first **edition** even had to be scrapped because it had the wrong date on!

Even so, the *Australian* began to roll off the presses in July 1964. It was Australia's very first national daily newspaper, and a landmark in the history of the country.

A new marriage

One day a beautiful young woman came to interview Murdoch for the Sydney *Mirror*'s staff magazine. She was Anna Torv, an ambitious journalist who was half Estonian and half Scottish. She and Rupert fell in love with each other very quickly. After his divorce from Pat they were married in April 1967. There were three children from Murdoch's marriage to Anna – Elisabeth, James and Lachlan.

Rupert and Anna Murdoch with their first child, Elisabeth.

INTO FLEET STREET

With his new wife Anna, Murdoch began to settle down. He bought an old stone house with thousands of acres of land near Canberra, where he installed an airstrip. He threw parties, collected modern paintings and farmed sheep and cattle. He even thought of running as the local member of parliament.

MURDOCH INVADES BRITAIN

But the most important thing in Murdoch's life was his business. His sights were now set outside Australia for the first time. In 1968, he had a phone call from London, informing him that the *News of the World* might be for sale. One **proprietor** was already itching to buy it – Robert Maxwell.

The *News of the World*, a Sunday newspaper, was the raciest of Britain's popular papers, and Maxwell fancied himself to be a media **tycoon**. Murdoch, in his turn, was desperate to get a foothold in the British market. But he had to move cautiously.

'I'm not an evil man. I'm here to help you if you want it. But I don't like to waste my time on dither.'
Murdoch to the owner of the *News of the World*, who had referred to Maxwell as 'an evil man'.

Robert Maxwell
(left) looks
confident,
Murdoch nervous
at the *News of
the World*
shareholders'
meeting. But
Murdoch won.

VICTORY OVER MAXWELL

He started talks with the owner of the newspaper. He suggested that he should become **managing director**, in return for 40 per cent of the company's shares. Murdoch's bid was recommended to the *News of the World* **shareholders** by the owner.

The contest was decided at a meeting of the shareholders. Murdoch gave a speech which was short and low-key. Maxwell was such an unpopular figure that when he rose to put his case, the listeners booed. Not surprisingly, the shareholders voted for the Australian in the end.

Taking over

Murdoch was not content just to be **managing director**. In a series of ruthless moves, he quickly took control of every aspect of the *News of the World*. He fired many of the old journalists, changed the **layout** and blocked the **editor's** orders. In the end, he sacked the editor, too!

Before the takeover, the paper had been selling fewer copies year by year and was down to a circulation of 6 million. Murdoch's answer was – as usual – to cut costs and add more sex and scandal. As usual, it worked. Within a few months, the **readership** had risen by 200,000 a week.

One of the big stories which Murdoch used to attract readers, September 1969.

NEWS OF THE WORLD

SUNDAY, SEPTEMBER 21, 1969.   No. 6,565   PRICE SEVENPENCE   6,517,000 copies sold last week

Morals AND Your Child
PAGES 5 and 6

World Exclusive

CHRISTINE KEELER —at last her FULL story

MURDOCH V MAXWELL: ROUND 2

Having a Sunday newspaper was a start. But Murdoch now had printing presses with nothing to do for six nights each week. He needed a daily paper to fill the gap.

As it happened, there was one for sale. The *Sun* had been launched in 1964 as a rival to the **downmarket** *Daily Mirror*. It had been a pitiful failure with a circulation plunging to around 1 million, and the owners were anxious to find a buyer.

Once again, the front-runner was Robert Maxwell. But his terms were rejected by the powerful **trade unions**, and he gave up his bid. Murdoch stepped in swiftly to take his place. After some tough bargaining, he landed the *Sun* for what now seems an amazingly small sum – between £250,000 and £500,000, depending on whether the paper survived. Murdoch had another bargain.

TRUTH AND BEAUTY AND JUSTICE?

The first **edition** of the new *Sun* appeared in November 1969. It contained a surprising statement from Rupert Murdoch himself. 'The most important thing to remember,' he wrote, 'is that the new *Sun* will still be a paper that CARES. The paper that cares – passionately – about truth and beauty and justice.'

He soon showed his concern for beauty by printing pictures of topless models. This was the birth of the famous 'Page Three Girl'. He also decided to change the paper's **format** from **broadsheet** to the smaller **tabloid** size.

THE RISING SUN

Within two years, the sales of the *Sun* had doubled and it had almost caught up with its rival, the *Daily Mirror*. In 1971 it was named as British Newspaper of the Year.

The main reason for this was the vast amount of money Murdoch spent on promoting the newspaper, especially advertising it on television. But it was also easier to read, with more space given to sex, sport, television and radio programmes, and competitions.

Changing sides

- Murdoch's politics are a strange mixture of Right and Left, Conservative and Labour. This was clear during the British General Election of 1970.

- On polling day, the *Sun* urged its readers to 'Vote Labour', the **left-wing** party led by Harold Wilson. But in the end the **right-wing** Conservatives won under the leadership of Ted Heath.

- The *Sun* immediately blamed the misleading **opinion polls** and switched sides. 'Well done, Ted Heath,' it said. 'The British love to see an outsider come surging up to pass the favourite.'

The *Sun* gets it wrong. The Tories won this election in 1970.

AMERICAN EXPANSION

Success in Britain was merely a stepping stone for Murdoch to reach the USA. This was the biggest and wealthiest market in the world – and it boasted over 1700 newspapers, as well as countless TV channels. Murdoch had been visiting the country for many years, asking questions and making contacts. Now he was ready to buy.

TRIP TO TEXAS

His first purchase was in 1973. Three newspapers in San Antonio, Texas, were just the price he could afford. They were being outsold by a bigger paper, the evening *Light*.

Murdoch used the same formula as before. He changed the **layout** and demanded sensational stories with attention-grabbing **headlines.** Some of these twisted the truth only a little, such as 'Uncle Tortures Pets With Hot Fork' and 'Armies of Insects Marching on SA'. Others were simply made up, especially the famous headline 'Killer Bees Move North'.

NATIONAL STAR

While the sales in San Antonio inched upwards, Murdoch was already busy on a bigger US project. This was the *National Star*. It was a weekly **tabloid**

NATIONAL **ENQUIRER** 15¢
Vol. 42, No. 4, October 1, 1967

Whatever Happened To Esther Williams?

A Leading American Scientist Says:

YES!
FLYING SAUCERS COME FROM OTHER PLANETS

'The Evidence That They Exist Is Overwhelming'

MOST IMPORTANT UFO PHOTO

A typically zany cover story for the *National Enquirer*, the US newspaper that Murdoch tried unsuccessfully to compete with.

paper, intended to compete directly with the old-established and hugely successful *National Enquirer*.

Murdoch planned to make most of the sales through supermarkets. He put all his energies into getting the *National Star* ready, and set aside a massive $5 million to **plug** it on television.

For once his magic touch failed. The supermarkets did not stock or sell enough copies, and the mixture of stories did not attract readers. TV advertising was stopped, and Murdoch gave up his challenge to the *National Enquirer*. But the *National Star* did not die. It was eventually re-born as a woman's weekly paper, and became very profitable.

THE BIG APPLE

The biggest and most powerful city in America was New York. If Murdoch was going to be taken seriously as a media **tycoon**, he had to have a major newspaper there. Luckily, one of the biggest – the *New York Post* – was for sale. The price was steep at $30 million, but Murdoch raised the money and the deal went through in November 1976.

At the same time, he was stalking another prey. This was a glossy and cleverly-written magazine called *New York*. When the journalists heard that Murdoch was going to be their new boss, many of them walked out. He had to do most of the work on the next issue himself.

PROTEST AND STRIKES

Murdoch had even bigger trouble at the *New York Post*. Many of the staff hated his brand of journalism, with its shouting **headlines,** invented stories and sexy photographs. There were protests and walkouts. Murdoch's answer was simple. He fired over 100 of the staff and replaced them with Australians.

'I can get better than you in a week. It's not your paper, it's my paper.'

Murdoch to a reporter who protested at his treatment of *New York Post* journalists, 1977.

He was just as cynical in dealing with other newspapers. When the printers went on strike in 1978, their actions brought all major New York papers to a halt. The newspaper owners asked Murdoch to be their spokesman. In spite of this, he secretly made his own deal with the print unions, and the *New York Post* was back on the streets well before its rivals.

SPENDING SPREE

Murdoch and his family had spent several years away from Australia. Now they returned, and seemed ready to settle down. Glad to be away from the snobbish atmosphere of Britain, he sent his children to Australian **boarding schools** and bought one of the biggest sheep stations in the land.

He bought plenty else besides. During 1979 he became owner of the company which ran Channel 10, one of Sydney's **commercial** TV stations. With partners, he gained the rights to run a lottery game throughout Australia. And he purchased Ansett Transport, which operated airlines and road transport and (more importantly) another TV channel.

There were failures, too. The most painful of these was the collapse of Murdoch's bid for the *Melbourne Herald*. He wanted the paper very badly, for it had once been run by his father. As a small boy, he had often visited the *Herald* offices, and felt its thrilling atmosphere. But other newspaper owners united to keep him out of Melbourne, and he gave up his bid.

The Times

All the same, the expansion of his empire went on. In 1980, Murdoch formed News Corporation as a

holding company for his many and varied businesses. Soon after this he flew to London to close a deal for *The Times* and *The Sunday Times*, thus becoming the most powerful figure in the British press.

These were by far the oldest and most respected newspapers he had bought. *The Times*, founded way back in 1785, was still seen as 'the top people's paper'. But it was losing a lot of money, largely due to a long-running battle between the print unions and the management. It was a problem which Murdoch was determined to solve.

Murdoch takes over the London Times in 1981.

BEATING THE UNIONS

By 1984, the Murdoch empire was enormous, churning out over 3 billion copies of newspapers a year. The *Sun* was the most important part of this, earning 40 per cent of News Corporation's profits. But the signs were not good. Sales were falling, and those of its great rival, the *Daily Mirror*, were rising. On top of this came the continuing losses at *The Times* and *The Sunday Times*.

THE NEW TECHNOLOGY

At this time most newspapers were still being produced in a very complex and old-fashioned way. **Type** was made on ancient **hot-metal** machines and set by hand. The whole process involved a large number of workers.

Old technology: how newspapers were prepared in the 1950s.

In Fleet Street, the traditional centre of the British newspaper industry, things were made much worse by the power of the print unions. They insisted on hundreds of extra workers being employed – at a huge cost in time and wages. Murdoch was outraged to discover that there were 6 men to each of his printing presses in New York, but 18 in London.

However, new production methods had been developed. Computer technology made it possible for journalists to set words in type themselves. This would make the printing process much more simple and efficient, and it would save the newspaper **proprietors** a staggering amount of money.

New technology: a computerized newsroom in Fleet Street in 1986.

THE BIG DECISION

Murdoch hatched a plan to make this happen. He decided to defeat the unions and build an entirely new plant to print his London papers. It would be at Wapping, part of the old London docklands next to Tower Bridge. To put the unions off the scent, Murdoch announced that he was going to produce a new daily paper at Wapping, aimed at London readers.

Working under cover

There was no London newspaper, of course. But Murdoch was so cunning that the print unions had no idea of what was really going on. The Wapping premises, once a factory and warehouse, had to be rebuilt. Secretly, Murdoch began to buy and install equipment at the site. Electricians (belonging to a separate union) had to travel in every day from faraway Southampton to fit the new equipment.

The whole project was a huge gamble. If the print unions had uncovered the scheme, they would have gone on strike immediately and News Corporation would have lost a fortune. This never happened.

Murdoch was able to complete his plans without a hitch. A fleet of 800 new trucks was bought, ready to distribute the Wapping papers. Coils of razor wire were fixed on top of the fences round the new plant to keep out troublemakers. Extra security guards were hired.

The storm breaks

Early in 1986, **editors** of the *Sun*, *The Times* and *News of the World* told their journalists about the move to Wapping. At first their reaction was of shock. Soon, however, most of them voted for the new deal.

The print unions were furious. New laws, passed by Margaret Thatcher's Conservative government, made it easier for employers to sack workers who went on strike. The News Corporation print workers knew that they had lost their jobs, and had nothing else to lose.

Thousands of them came to the gates of the Wapping plant to picket, and prevent the journalists from getting into work. There were fights. When riot police were called, the strikers threw stones and bottles at them. One night, more than 250 people were injured.

Demonstrators at Wapping push over barriers in a clash with police.

A WAPPING VICTORY

Murdoch's careful planning brought him complete success. Early in 1987, the unions agreed to a deal – the print workers lost their jobs but received a payout in compensation. The size of the workforce dropped from 2,000 to 570. Newspaper profits began to rise almost overnight.

All the same, Murdoch had become a hate figure for many Britons. They believed that he was a bully who had used the law to put people out of work. Scores of valuable journalists resigned from the The Times and Sun in protest against his actions.

Becoming American

'Who can say that I am not a good Australian or a patriotic one?' asked Murdoch in 1979. At that time he was fighting to take over Sydney's TV Channel 10, and had to show that he was a loyal Australian resident.

Six years later, he stood up at a ceremony in New York and promised his allegiance to the US flag. He thus gave up his Australian citizenship and became an American. This time, he was in the process of starting a TV network in the USA, and had to show that he was a loyal American citizen.

Many were outraged in both America and Australia. One US journalist wrote: 'Murdoch is allowed to become a citizen while we're turning away people who are running from death squads or starvation.'

MOVING INTO THE MOVIES

The famous film logo for Twentieth-Century Fox, in which Murdoch bought a half share in 1985.

The battles at Wapping had come at a hectic time for Murdoch. He had just completed two of the biggest deals of his life. For some $250 million, he bought a half-share in the major Hollywood film and TV company Twentieth-Century Fox. Then he snapped up several independent US TV stations from a company called Metromedia for a further $2 billion. Both these enterprises were combined in a massive new media and entertainment company – Fox Incorporated.

SATELLITE WARS

The Murdoch spending spree showed no signs of stopping. He bought – at the second attempt – the *Melbourne Herald* which his father had once run. He took over the *South China Morning Post* in Hong Kong. He purchased the US book publisher Harper and Row and took control of London book publishers William Collins. He even bought another British newspaper, the middle market daily *Today*.

In 1988, Murdoch went further and splashed out $3 billion on a US listings magazine called *TV Guide*. This was a staggering price to pay, but *TV Guide* was easily the USA's biggest selling magazine. It gave details of all TV programmes nationwide and was very popular with advertisers.

Enter the Simpsons

Meanwhile Fox Incorporated had launched Fox TV, a new television network in the USA. It was an instant success, thanks largely to the first appearance of *The Simpsons*. This chaotic cartoon family quickly became cult viewing with young Americans.

THE BIRTH OF SKY

The purchase of *TV Guide* was a big risk. Now Murdoch took an even bigger one. He announced that he was creating a brand new television network which would be beamed down to Britain by **satellite**. It would cost £40 million to develop, and was to be called Sky TV.

Murdoch launches his satellite television service, Sky TV, in 1988. Plans had already been drawn up for another satellite network, British Satellite Broadcasting (BSB). Murdoch's Sky was a direct challenge to it. The two rivals raced each other to get ready for launch, buying up American TV shows and rights to Hollywood films. Sky, driven on by Murdoch's energy, went on air first, well ahead of BSB.

A STICKY START

Murdoch had two priceless advantages over his rivals. For a start, his **satellite** network was already on air. BSB was still bogged down with technical problems which would put it more than a year behind Sky. Then there were the Murdoch newspapers. The *Sun*, *News of the World* and *Today* could give endless **plugs** to Sky in what was really a free promotional campaign.

All the same, the new network was largely ignored. Few people watched it, because they had not bought the 'dish' aerials needed to receive the

The owner of Sky TV takes a tour of the newsroom with company chairman Andrew Neil.

satellite signal. This in turn discouraged anyone from paying for advertising time. Soon, News Corporation was losing £2 million each week through Sky. It looked like a disaster.

RE-LAUNCH

Murdoch's next step was typical. 'It's my big gamble, and I'd better see it through,' he said. Instead of retreating and cutting his losses, he pushed forward. Sky dishes were not selling in the shops? Well then, he would give them away! Salesmen also toured the streets offering cut-price rental deals on Sky equipment. Slowly the army of Sky watchers began to grow.

'Mr Murdoch has a position of unique power in British life that no other Western country would permit a foreigner to hold.'
BSB directors, referring to Murdoch's control of television stations and national newspapers, 1990.

This was a very anxious period for Murdoch. He had invested a vast amount in his satellite channel. But BSB was ready to go on air at last in the spring of 1990, and had already begun a massive advertising campaign. And there clearly was not room for both of them.

MERGER

If Sky was doing badly, BSB was doing even worse. Few people were buying the company's 'squarial' receiver systems, and it was losing over £8 million a week, four times as much as Sky. Something had to be done – and fast.

The obvious answer was to combine the two **satellite** networks. Murdoch held a series of talks with the BSB directors. He even went to Downing Street to tell the prime minister, Margaret Thatcher, what was going on. At last a **merger** was announced. The new company was to be called BSkyB, and Murdoch would own 50 per cent of it.

INTO THE EAST

Murdoch now had a firm grip on satellite broadcasting in Britain and much of Western Europe. He also had plans to extend his power into Eastern Europe, which was slowly emerging from

The long arm of News Corporation: a satellite TV dish in rural Poland.

decades under Communist rule. There were major business opportunities in countries like Hungary. Murdoch quickly snapped up two newspapers here – the weekly *Reform* and the daily *Mai Nap* – and promoted his Sky TV channels.

CRISIS AT CHRISTMAS

By 1990, Murdoch had been expanding and buying for more than 30 years. Murdoch had made most of his purchases by borrowing money from banks. His debt was now an astonishing $7.5 billion and rising.

It was a bad time for the whole world economy. Bankers were demanding payment from their debtors. If Murdoch failed to get his debts **rolled over** for another period, the vast company he had built up would fall to pieces.

The crunch came just before Christmas 1990. A US bank was refusing to roll over the News Corporation debt and insisting that Murdoch repaid them what he owed immediately. His entire empire was on the brink of disaster.

Murdoch made one final telephone call, begging the bank official to change his mind. It worked. The loan would be renewed, and News Corporation was saved.

Cutting back

A year after the cash crisis of 1990, Murdoch's fortunes were looking much healthier. He had raised money by selling off several of his **assets**, including a group of US magazines, and by selling shares in some of his businesses. He had cut costs throughout the company, even though this meant firing over 5,000 of his employees. All the extra money went to paying off his most urgent loans.

Looking to the east

But this did not stop Murdoch from pursuing new deals. The boldest of these took him to China, the biggest untapped market in the world with an enormous population. In partnership with the country's major newspaper, the *People's Daily*, he set up an Internet service. This allowed Chinese people to access foreign news and prepared the way for News Corporation's **satellite** TV to be introduced.

Sky high

The fortunes of struggling BSkyB began to change, too. The company drew in viewers by introducing a number of successful new TV channels. Among them was Gold Plus, which showed well-loved old programmes (including 3,000 vintage episodes of the soap opera Coronation Street).

Suddenly, the satellite network was making money. In 1992, it had lost £20 million: a year later it made a whopping profit of £62 million. By 1996, over 5 million homes in Britain had signed up to receive BSkyB by satellite or cable.

Sport was the major attraction. In a series of sensational deals, the network bought up exclusive rights to big sporting events, notably boxing title fights and football. In 1992, BSkyB won the rights to show live Premier League football action. The growing hold of BSkyB worried many people, who believed that Rupert Murdoch had far too much power.

Murdoch is shown the stadium of the Los Angeles Dodgers, a US baseball team he bought in 1998.

Opinions on Rupert Murdoch

Rupert Murdoch has been called a lot of rude names. The British satirical magazine *Private Eye* always refers to him as 'The Dirty Digger' ('dirty' because of his newspapers' liking for sleaze, and 'digger' because it is a slang term for an Australian). A Chicago journalist called him 'a greedy, money-grubbing, power-seeking, status-climbing cad'.

When he took over the *New York Post*, *Time* magazine put him on its cover. He was shown as King Kong, grabbing control of the media and scaring New Yorkers. To many people, he appears to be an utterly ruthless operator who believes that money will get him anything.

His cynical methods of doing business have certainly affected the way TV and newspaper executives work. The manager of the rival New York *Daily News* changed his tactics once

Hounding by tabloid photographers was blamed for the tragic death of Diana, Princess of Wales.

News Corporation arrived. 'In Murdoch's world there are no rules,' he said. 'Now that he has shown how he works, we'll do it, too.'

On the other hand, many people admire him as a spectacularly successful businessman. Other top media proprietors name him as their most impressive competitor. 'Rupert doesn't chisel,' said one, meaning that once he has agreed a deal and a price he will stick to it.

In private conversations Murdoch can also be charming and courteous, concentrating all his attention on the person he is talking to. He inspires fierce loyalty from many of his staff. He will pay huge salaries to hire someone he really wants but then he will instantly fire employees who disappoint him.

WHAT MAKES MURDOCH RUN?

Murdoch rarely relaxes. He is driven on relentlessly by his ambition. His aim is simple and obvious – to build up the first and biggest truly global broadcasting and entertainment operation. His astonishing success shows how hard he works and how cunning he is.

But what makes him do it? At an age when most people are thinking of retirement, Murdoch shows no signs of slowing down. To some people, his motives are simple. One American journalist defined two of them: 'to beat his father, Keith. And to run the world.'

Certainly, he had enormous admiration for his father. 'A good father and son relationship is one of the best experiences in life', he once wrote. He may have had some surprisingly left-wing views while his father was alive, but after his death he swiftly changed into a conservative. What's more, in building up a newspaper empire he was carrying out his father's wishes. Three of Rupert Murdoch's children – Elisabeth, James and Lachlan – have in turn followed him into the business. James is head of Star TV and Lachlan works for News Corporation. Elisabeth has recently left New Corporation after many years.

Sayonara

A rare moment of relaxation for Murdoch, on board US racing yacht Sayonara.

How does Rupert Murdoch see himself? He makes few personal statements, and keeps his private life as private as possible (not a luxury his newspapers allow other famous figures). He is also a strong, but conventional Christian.

Murdoch makes no secret of his heavy burden of responsibility. 'As a **proprietor** I'm the one who in the end is responsible for the success or failure of my papers' he said when he bought the *News of the World* in 1969.

Occasionally, he has let slip phrases which reveal his own view of his character. These show a gigantic confidence in his own abilities. He once boasted to a journalist 'I bet, if I was going to be shot at dawn, I could get out of it.' So far, he has succeeded.

Rupert Murdoch – Timeline

1931 Rupert Murdoch born to a wealthy family near Melbourne, Australia

1942 Begins boarding at Geelong Grammar School

1948 Leaves school and works as a cub reporter on *Melbourne Herald*

1950 Goes to Worcester College, Oxford

1952 Death of his father: returns to Australia for funeral

1953 Leaves Oxford with a third-class degree; works as a sub-editor on the London *Daily Express*; returns to Australia to take charge of News Limited, his father's company

1955 Begins purchase of minor papers in Australia

1956 Marries air hostess Patricia Booker

1958 Granted licence to run TV Channel 9 in Adelaide

1959 Daughter Prudence born

1960 Buys *Mirror* newspapers in Sydney

1964 Starts national daily the *Australian* in Canberra

1967 Divorce from wife Patricia; marries journalist Anna Torv

1968 Buys *News of the World* in London

1969 Buys the *Sun*

1973 Buys *San Antonio Express* and *News*

1976 Buys *New York Post*

1979 Buys controlling shares of Ansett Transport Industries; gains the right to run Australian national lottery

1980 Forms News Corporation as holding company; buys the *The Times* and *The Sunday Times*

1985 Buys half-share in 20th Century Fox; becomes US citizen

1986 Moves his London newspaper operations to Wapping; print workers picket the Wapping complex

1987 Many print workers lose their jobs after deal with print unions; Murdoch buys US book publisher Harper & Row

1988 Pays $3 billion for *TV Guide* in US

1989 Launch of Sky TV in the UK; buys British book-publisher William Collins

1990 Merges with BSB to form BSkyB

1993 Sets up Star TV, a pan-Asian TV service based in Hong Kong

1995 Clinches deal to launch Internet service in China

1996 BSkyB screens exclusive pay-per-view coverage of world title boxing match

1999 Divorce from second wife Anna; marries TV executive Wendi Deng

Murdoch with his third wife, Wendi Deng, a former vice-president of Star TV.

GLOSSARY

asset something of value that a person owns, such as property or equipment

boarding school a school where pupils live during term time

broadsheet a newspaper with a large format

class system the way society can be divided into types, or classes, of people – often depending on their wealth

commercial financed by advertising or an advert itself

cub reporter a young trainee journalist

digital TV a system of sending TV signals using binary code

downmarket something inferior in quality and/or style

edition a particular printing of a newspaper; each day's paper may be altered to reflect changing news and thus produced in different editions

editor someone in charge of the content of a newspaper

format the size and layout of a publication

headline the short line above a news or feature story which gives a brief summary of what the story is about

holding company a company which has control over other companies

hot-metal a method of printing using metal type which is cast into shape when it is heated to melting point

layout the way in which pictures and stories are arranged on a newspaper or magazine page

left-wing wanting to reform society, redistribute wealth and make people more equal

licence official permission to do or own something, usually in the form of a document

managing director someone who has control over an organization

merger the combining of two or more companies

opinion poll a way of finding out how the public feels on a topic by asking questions of a sample group of people

plugs frequent mentions of something, to help advertise it

proprietor a person who own something

racism belief that some races are better than others

readership the people who read a particular newspaper or magazine

right-wing favouring conservative policies and the retention of a class system

roll over to allow someone a longer time to pay off a debt

satellite a man-made object which orbits the Earth, and which can be used to relay TV and radio signals

share a part of the stock of a company which can be bought and sold

shareholder a person who owns a share of a company

socialism a system of politics in which goods and power are shared out equally

sub-editor a journalist who corrects and alters a reporter's text to make it ready for printing or broadcasting

tabloid a newspaper with a small format, usually giving news in a condensed form

trade union an organized group of workers in a particular trade or profession

tycoon a wealthy and powerful business person

type a block of metal or wood with raised letters which is inked and pressed on paper to print words

INDEX